My World

JOBS IN MY NEIGHBORHOOD

By Gladys Rosa-Mendoza • Illustrations by Ann Iosa

WINDMILL BOOKS

New York

Published in 2011 by Windmill Books, LLC
303 Park Avenue South, Suite # 1280, New York, NY 10010-3657

Adaptations to North American Edition © 2011 Windmill Books, LLC
First published by me+mi publishing, inc. © 2007
Text and illustrations copyright © me+mi publishing, inc., 2007

CREDITS:
Author: Gladys Rosa-Mendoza
Illustrator: Ann Iosa

Library of Congress Cataloging-in-Publication Data

Rosa-Mendoza, Gladys.
  Jobs in my neighborhood / by Gladys Rosa-Mendoza ; illustrated by Ann Iosa. — School & library ed.
      p. cm. — (My world)
  Includes bibliographical references and index.
  ISBN 978-1-60754-952-9 (library binding) — ISBN 978-1-61533-037-9 (pbk.) — ISBN 978-1-61533-038-6 (6-pack)
  1. Occupations—Juvenile literature. I. Iosa, Ann. II. Title.
  HF5381.2.R66 2010
  331.702—dc22
                              2009054407

Manufactured in the United States of America

For more great fiction and nonfiction, go to www.windmillbooks.com.

CPSIA Compliance Information: Batch #S10W: For further information contact Windmill Books, New York, New York at 1-866-478-0556.

Contents

Every day, people are doing jobs in this neighborhood.

There are police officers helping kids to cross the street safely.

There are firefighters helping
a cat that is stuck in a tree.

Over here is a bus driver
taking kids to school.

Over there is a gardener
planting flowers in a yard.

A barber is cutting a boy's blond hair at the barber shop.

A veterinarian is checking a dog's ears.

This teacher is helping his students learn to read.

That doctor is giving
a little girl a checkup.

This postal worker is delivering the mail to people's houses.

These garbage collectors are picking up the trash and taking it to a landfill.

A librarian is helping a girl
find a book at the library.

This mechanic is fixing a
green car at his garage.

This grocer is selling some carrots at his store.

This baker has made fresh loaves of bread at her bakery.

There are lots of jobs being done in this neighborhood.

Read More!

Nonfiction

Kenney, Karen Latchana. *Mail Carriers at Work.* Minneapolis, MN: Magic Wagon, 2009.

Minden, Cecilia. *Veterinarians.* Mankato, MN: Child's World, 2006.

Fiction

Mayer, Mercer. *This Is My Town.* New York: HarperCollins, 2008.

Slater, Dashka. *Firefighters in the Dark.* New York: Houghton Mifflin, 2006.

Learn More!

 There are about 1.5 million fires in the United States every year.

 Many veterinarians take care of pets like dogs and cats. Some vets care mostly for farm animals like horses, cows, and pigs.

 The biggest library in the world is the Library of Congress in Washington, D.C.

What jobs do your parents do in your neighborhood? What job do you want to do when you grow up?

Words to Know

barber (BAR-bur) a person who cuts people's hair

gardener (GAR-den-ur) a person who grows plants

firefighters (FY-er-fy-turz) people who put out fires

grocer (GROW-shur) a person who works in a grocery store

garbage collector (GAR-buj kuh-lek-tur) a person who picks up people's garbage

librarian (ly-BREH-ree-an) a person who works in a library

mechanic (meh-KAN-ik)
a person who fixes cars

postal worker (POHS-tul
wur-kur) someone who works at the post
office and delivers mail

neighborhood (NAY-bur-hood)
the place where many people live and
work together

teacher (TEE-chur) someone
who works in a school

police officers (poh-LEES
ah-fih-surs) people who protect us

veterinarian (veh-ter-NAYR-
ree-un) a doctor who takes care
of animals

Index

Web Sites

For Web resources related to the subject of this book, go to:
www.windmillbooks.com/weblinks and select this book's title